TRAIN TO COMPETE

TRAIN TO COMPETE

HOW TO COMPETE WITH YOUR TEAM BY TRAINING 2-3 DAYS A WEEK

GUIDE FOR FOOTBALL COACHES

Álvaro Bracamonte Martins

ISBN: 979-8-456-70580-8

© 2021 Álvaro Bracamonte Martins.

All rights reserved.

No part of this work may be reproduced in any form or by any means, electronic, mechanical, photocopying, recording or otherwise, without the prior written permission of the author.

ÁLVARO BRACAMONTE MARTINS

A Physical Education, Sports and Recreation graduate from the University of Carabobo (Venezuela). Level II soccer coach in Spain (Sports Technician, Medium Grade, Final level) having studied at CENAFE. Participates as a teacher in the Carabobo State Soccer Association coaches course-CEFUTBOL (FVF, Venezuela). A staff member at CD Galapagar, a senior team in Spain's 3rd Division, Madrid group 7, he works with formative football in different categories.

ÍNDICE

Introduction	9
Chapter I Planning Training Sessions with Purpose	15
Chapter II Explanation, Demonstration and Correction in Training	27
Chapter III How to Develop Your Team Faster	37
Chapter IV Offensive Game Styles: According to Player Characteristics and External Factors	47
Chapter V Defensive Game Styles: According to Players Charateristics	59
Chapter VI Ready to Compete	67
Chapter VII Planning and Managing Football Matches	81
Chapter VIII Analyzing Matches Objectively	93
Chapter IX Now What?	105
Chapter X Final Comments and Bibliography	111

INTRODUCTION

PREFACE

This book looks for a way to train a football team to achieve an optimal level of competitiveness. From professional, personal, and international experience, a brief introduction to the subject of the book is made.

Each point of the text is born from professional, personal, and international experience and practice.

Subsequently, a short critical note is attached that specifies some thematic details that are important to understand the overall goal of the text.

INTRODUCTION

Is it possible to be competitive with a football team by only training 2 days a week?

Before I answer, I want to say that: as a coach, you must doubt everything that everyone says about football, **because there is NO absolute truth**.

Based on that idea, this book intends to provide my knowledge and experience after having trained as a coach in Spain. However, I have learned from many coaches, but they have also learned from others. And this is the chain of learning: each with their own beliefs and experiences.

You will see that there are tools, ideas and strategies, but they are conditioned by my experiences, by my education, by how I have been taught and by the way I see football.

By doubting everything, you begin to draw your own conclusions. You can agree more or less with everything that is written here, but my proposal is only one of many that exist. **It is about adding ideas, experiences, beliefs and finally, building your own**.

I had my belief about this discipline, and it changed in a few months...

3 years ago, I thought I knew a lot as a football coach, I had been managing at different levels in 2 different countries for 8 years. After having read books, exercise guides and having done the training course in Venezuela, I felt confident in starting down a new path in this world.

To continue learning, I came to Spain, a country that loves football and has high-level coaches. I decided to start my academic training and completed Level 1 as a football coach in Madrid (UEFA B). I must admit that I did not learn much, which for me was good news because it meant that I had "good" previous knowledge, especially in grassroots football training.

Months later, in June 2018, I decided to take Level 2 (UEFA A) in a CENAFE intensive. That changed my whole perspective on football; everything I believed up to that moment, changed. Most of the teachers just provide information from already existing books, but they did not deepen or make you reflect on anything. However, one of them, Álvaro Gómez-Rey, provided us with information and questions to the point that I began to wonder if I really knew anything about football.

I began to analyse details that, although they were obvious, often went unnoticed. It helped me to think about the reason for each of the situations and how to work in professional football to adapt it to amateur football.

I liked his classes so much that I proposed to work with him, and he accepted. Thanks to Álvaro and that drive that helped me to continue training month after month, I decided to write this book to guide other coaches to be competitive with any amateur team by training only 2 days a week.

Before I thought: "I don't have time", we only train two days a week, and how am I going to be competitive with an amateur team? I believed that it could not be done, that it was unfeasible. I was wrong.

I have led a youth team, we trained two days a week on half a pitch with minimum resources and in just 60 minutes (50 minutes if you take away the warm-up and organizing materials). We were promoted for the first time in the history of the Canal. **Promotion is not important, because many factors played a part, but they played with good judgment**, despite the little training time we had.

Going back to the original question: is it possible to be competitive with a football team by only training 2 days a week?

YES, you can compete if you dedicate your time to what is important. In other words, we must stop wasting precious minutes on things that are less important in the little training time we have.

COMMENTS ON THIS EDITION

This book offers a comprehensive look at different ways of seeing and understanding football. It aims to analyse, based on personal experiences, lived and learned from the perspective of a football coach, what his vision of the game is and what his personal learning journey has begotten as useful material on which to reflect for an audience interested in the subject. You must train to be competitive, but, as discussed throughout this text, there are ways to achieve this with specific strategies.

Through different passages, divided into chapters, a series of concrete methods of play is proposed. Some of the problems addressed are: how to attack, how to defend, how to communicate with the players, how to face a defeat, how a young player can evolve, how effective communication can be achieved with children, young people and adult football players for a successful training session.

Ultimately, what is proposed in this text is a review, marked by a highly personal touch, of what football is and how an adequate training strategy can achieve the best development of footballers in training, as well as those who aspire to dedicate themselves to this sport from the bench as a coach of a team.

CHAPTER I

PLANNING TRAINING SESSIONS WITH PURPOSE

They talk about planning football training as comprehensively as possible.

This is an introductory chapter that proposes the theoretical keys that will accompany you throughout the book. There is talk of different types of game phases (between offensive, defensive).

In the same way, some tips on training sessions, games, conversations with the players that stimulate the coach and the player as part of a team are given.

INTRODUCTION

What does purposeful training planning mean? It could be a broad debate with diverse opinions and ideas from many coaches. But, without a doubt, **we must focus on competitiveness**, bearing in mind the factors that influence the training of our players and the training time available; whether they are children, teenagers, or adults.

This point is not intended to talk about planning training in terms of practical exercises, for that there are already books, guides, and information on the internet. However, there is something basic that we coaches tend to forget because we do not consider or do not know all the important factors for the optimal development of the players.

I will mention some ideas to develop a plan with purpose, focused on the competitiveness and how, in my opinion, a session should be planned.

I will divide this point into amateur football and grassroots football to clarify important aspects of each.

STRATEGIES

Amateur football

Session objective

What are you going to teach? What do you want them to learn or improve that day? What do you want to convey? There are long-term and short-term goals, but each session must have some objective that you want to reach through exercises.

With the objective **you must keep in mind which of the 4 phases of the game you want to focus on at the weekend**. It can be the offensive phase, defensive phase, offensive transition, or defensive transition. Let me briefly explain them:

- **Offensive phase**: This is when your team has the ball and is taking the initiative in the game. You can attack through possession (combinatorial attack) or direct attack.

- **Defensive phase**: This is where the opponent has the ball and the objective of your team can be to press, contain or a mixture, to try to steal the ball.

- **Offensive transition**: Also known as the defence-attack transition. This is when your team recovers the ball and prepares to attack with the possibility of having a defensively disorganized rival. This can be done by counterattacking or by maintaining possession.

- **Defensive transition**: Also known as attack-defence transition. As opposed to the previous transition, this is where your team loses the ball and must reorganise to defend. This can be done by pressing (trying to recover it as soon as possible), or by gathering the team behind the ball, to defend in a specific area of the field (retreat). A combination of both can be carried out.

The objectives that you set in the session can be focused on specific micro-aspects of some phase of the game. For example: "body profile for controlling the ball", which is a sub-sub-principle of ball control, of the offensive phase.

Also, we refer to macro-aspects such as: "team organization after losing the ball", which is the beginning of the defensive transition.

Of course, you have to give all the objectives a purpose according to their ages. They need to be easily understandable and transferable to the pitch.

To explain what the principles and sub-principles of the game phases consist of, I will give an example of what I have just explained:

- **Phase**: offensive (attacking)

- **Principle**: ball control

- **Sub-principle**: oriented control

- **Sub-subprinciple**: body profile

The principle is what you want to be practiced in the training session. However, in controlling the ball several things can be worked: neutral control, oriented control, semi-stop control, control with the thigh, etc.; that would correspond to the sub principle. And finally, the sub-sub principle is something more specific; In this example it is the body profile, since we want to note that, prior to performing the targeted control, our players are positioned comfortably enough to perceive the opponent and receive the ball to turn.

This is a way of training an action in detail, but many sub-principles can be practiced at the same time. You can make a list of all the

The exercises must be progressive

sub-sub-principles that go into each action to have more resources when planning.

After learning the level of your players, you should know whether to start from scratch, if you should enhance certain qualities or if it is necessary to delve into technical-tactical aspects. It is useless to carry out a 6v6 task with 4 mini goals and give complex instructions (make 7 passes as a team before scoring a goal) if your players do not master the basic technical principles. **You must design progressive tasks for the team level.**

Sometimes the same task that can be complex can be adjusted by changing the number of players, adding wild cards, modifying the dimensions, time, repetitions, etc. It is important that, **if they do not know what they are doing and it is not related to what they can do in a match, they will not progress optimally.**

Exercise design

When I started in the world of coaching, I looked for exercises on the internet and in books, that way I had tools to plan my sessions. The problem is that most of these exercises have different purposes, and **you must adapt them to what you are looking for with your team.**

Ideally, when you have more resources from other trainers, you learn to do the exercises yourself. Finding drills in videos usually takes a long time, and if you do them, instead of taking them from books or the Internet, it will increase your creativity, your speed when planning and give you more resources for the future. I recommend you put them somewhere where you can find them later.

Here is a template of exercises with which I usually plan training sessions. I usually save them according to the type of exercise and, when I need to modify some nuance or repeat it in the session, I look for them. They make my job easier.[1]

Modify tasks during the session

During the season there will be times when some activity you have planned does not go as expected. Either because they don't understand it, because of the dimensions, the rules, etc. Experience and practice will give you the resources to modify exercises during training.

When you want to inject more complexity into the planning of the session, **think about a possible adaptation of the exercise in case it does not work**, above all for tasks with many stimuli to perceive, confusing rotations or that requires a lot of precision in the execution.

Number of tasks and duration

There is a lot of information on this point, and I do not consider there to be a single formula. Ideally, and what many coaches agree on, is that per training you perform **between 3 and 4 tasks** so that your players have time to master the activities. Of course, you must consider the time depending on the exercise. If they are analytical tasks, try to reduce the duration since too much time on the same activity of this type can bore your players.

A 60-minute session could be: greeting, warm-up (game) 10 minutes; analytical task or combined action (dribbling, control and passing, with variations) 12 minutes; then a positional games task (with variations) 18 minutes; finish with a 20-minute game with conditions. This always includes the explanation and organization of the exercise.

---

1   See *http://www.mediafire.com/file/ajmpzqz33mm8i3h/Template.pptx/file*

Therefore, including more tasks will cause you to waste training time explaining to the players, organizing the materials, and less time for the execution of the activity you want to carry out. It is more practical to put variants of the same exercise than having to incorporate a different exercise to practice the same thing.

Play in training (matches, mini matches)

Although it is logical, I have seen that many coaches tend to structure training sessions without including games or mini games in some sessions. The players want to have fun and the biggest stimulus for fun is playing matches. I don't mean that we are going to give them a ball to play all training. No. **The match must make sense based on the objectives set**, that is, we can give instructions or modifications so that situations arise where we want the team to improve.

So, including games or mini games in our planning is necessary. Also, **what do your players do at the weekend? Play.** So, it makes sense to make them play in training, and more so if they only train 2 or 3 days a week.

Mix the teams up. Don't have the first XI all together

When a player doesn't know who will start, he usually tries harder during practice. If you divide the teams into starters vs. substitutes, you are giving information to the players about the weekend, demotivating some players and lowering the performance of group training.

The ideal situation is to mix starters and substitutes. In addition, you will reach match levels during the session and will make most of the players work hard to earn their spot.

Planning with names: Make the most of your time

Write the names of your players in the planning of drills where they are required to be divided into groups or teams, either for small exercises or matches. This idea facilitates the development of the session because you can have them organized in advance and not waste time separating them by levels during training.

The disadvantage is that we normally work with amateur football or grassroots football, and we cannot exactly control the players who are going to train each day. However, we can plan with some idea of who will be there.

What I did at some clubs was ask the players to please let me know during the day when they were not going to be able to attend training sessions.

At first, it's difficult. Some will forget to tell you, but you can remind them until they get used to it. Explain that your plans influence the number of players there will be. Over time, you will know exactly who will attend except for specific situations that may occur.

If they are children, you should ask the parents to notify you privately

As a coach, you will often have to change what you had planned. Either by changing the number of players (this is common), by adapting the spaces or even by the weather (if it is very cold, change passive activities to more active ones, or if it is raining, etc.). But, if you know more or less how many players are going to attend training, you will need to improvise less and the planning will be easier to execute or modify to meet the objectives.

Grassroots football

I have added this section to get the most out of your players and enhance their qualities, even if they are children. Grassroots football is not focused on competing, except in certain categories and ages. But, in addition to the previous points, we must consider:

Sensitive stages of motor development

If you work with grassroots football, you should know at least a little, what the sensitive stages are, or also known as sensitive phases in the development of children, to enhance the physical qualities of your players, considering their age.

However, these are standard parameters and are used as general criteria for the development of children and teenagers, although not all children of the same age have the same physical development. For example, we will find cases of 10-year-old children with motor development of 7- or 8-year-olds.

So, you should not only focus on a single point of the sensitive phase, but also consider the type of development of your group to start planning.

Is it decisive to know the sensitive stages? For me, it is important to know how a player can be empowered by stimulating their physical qualities (**I am not talking about working on physical preparation with a child**). However, it is not decisive because you can become a good youth football coach without knowing the sensitive phases. In addition, the general development of a child is not only achieved by practicing a sport 2 hours a week.

Here is a table, as a reference, of the sensitive phases. The bars show what we should strengthen according to age[2]:

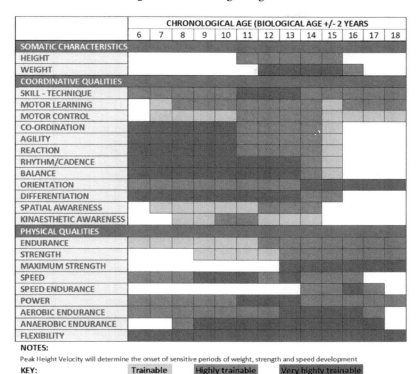

Know the current level of development of your players compared to other teams

It is normal that the first few years of grassroots football generate many doubts. You could have a team that you do not know if it is at

---

2   See *https://worldtenniscommunity.com/courses/itf-coaching-beginner-and-intermediate-players-course-introduction-to-physical-conditioning/lessons/the-development-phases-and-sensitive-periods/topic/the-development-phases-and-sensitive-periods/*

TRAIN TO COMPETE

the level of development that it should for their age. Although, if you compare your players with others of the same age, **you will be able to see the difference in execution times and body gestures.** From there, you will see if your team is average or if you need to be patient with the basics until they solidify it.

If you already have experience working with children, you can easily detect it by performing control and passing exercises, numerical equality situations, possession games, mini-games or matches.

Divide groups by levels of development

If you have a team with a big difference in level of development, when planning the session, **you should focus on making groups of equal or similar levels**, even in drills with a small number of players.

For example: 1vs1, 2vs2, 2vs1, 3vs3, etc. In this way, everyone will be able to participate in the activities with the possibility of having the ball, stealing it and having fun. If there is a lot of inequality, there will always be a team that beats another without the possibility of competing or improving.

CHAPTER II

EXPLANATION, DEMONSTRATION AND CORRECTION IN TRAINING

HOW TO COMMUNICATE TO BE COMPETITIVE

Appropriate training that reviews all offensive and defensive strategies is essential for a football match. However, this is impossible without proper communication with the players.

Explanations, demonstrations, and corrections are different methods that the trainer can use to convey their ideas.

The next chapter speaks, from personal experience and a concrete perspective of the game, on how communication can help to improve the individual and collective gameplay of the player and the team.

INTRODUCTION

When I started as a football coach, I was 19 years old, they gave me a team of 4-5 year old boys and I had no experience in leading groups, but I did have many years as a player. I thought it would not be difficult to explain some drills, but at first it was difficult. Perhaps I knew what I wanted to explain, but not how to do it, not the tone of voice, or the timing, or how to capture the attention of the group, or where I should be positioned during the exercise or what to emphasize when giving corrections. This I learned over time.

Knowing how to communicate, explain, correct, observe, and intervene, generates confidence and seriousness in the players (especially with teens and adults). If you do not know how to communicate and explain, it is difficult for training to have a positive transference to the game.

Just to reflect, have you ever been taught how to explain the exercises? Where do you place yourself to do them and why? What are the important aspects to consider? How should you make corrections?

When do you give positive feedback? If you know, it is because you have already had experience as a coach.

If you have already been working in the world of football for a while, surely you will have mastered some points that I mention below, but if you take away one or two important things that complement your training sessions, I will have fulfilled my objective.

STRATEGIES

Explanation and demonstration of the exercises

Organise the players and put yourself in the right place

Once you have the materials for the exercise on the field and the players are in the ideal positions for the drill, you should place yourself somewhere everyone can hear your explanation, or at the start, if you are going to demonstrate the exercise. After explaining it, **you should be positioned where you can observe as much as possible and be close enough to make corrections or give feedback**.

It is a common mistake for many coaches to position themselves at one end or the beginning of some activity that does not require a demonstration, without taking into account the players furthest away. If your voice is not loud or if they are distracted, they will surely not hear you.

Prepared material

For your drills, you must have the materials that you are going to use, not only those that you put on the field to mark areas or exercises, but you should also have more balls ready because, if you lose one, it is advisable to have another one ready quickly so the drill is not interrupted for long. **Continuity is one of the keys to achieving the objectives in each session**. Also, bibs (vests) in case you have to change a player's team or add wild cards in any activity.

If an exercise lasts for 18 minutes in total, including the explanation, breaks and repetitions, and each time a ball is lost 10-15 seconds are lost to go and get it and restart the activity, the productive time of the task is very short.

Explanation and demonstration

To explain an exercise to your players, I have decided to break it down into 4 different ways depending on the situation:

- Explanation without demonstration.

- Explanation with your demonstration.

- Explanation with player demonstration.

- Mixed explanation.

- **Explanation without demonstration**: I usually use it for exercise that the players know or are easy to perform and do not require complex decision making.

- **Explanation with your demonstration**: when you explain and at the same time demonstrate everything the players have to do. This makes it easier for you to capture their attention, for the exercise to be understood and for them to copy you.

  It is usually done in activities that require a sequence of individual actions and of course is age-dependent. It is often used with children because imitation is easier for them to understand and it gets their attention.

- **Explanation with player demonstration**: while you are explaining what the players should do, one or more of them will carry out the action you are asking for. I usually use it when they have already established or know the concepts of the task they are going to carry out.

- **Mixed explanation**: This is the most important, most trainers commonly use it. This is the combination of 2 or 3 of the explanations mentioned above. For example, you can start the explanation of a part of the drill without demonstrating it and then, when it is necessary to clarify something important or something that they do not know, explain, and demonstrate that action. Or have them demonstrate a part of the exercise while you explain it to them. Then you would demonstrate a specific part because it is important in your objective.

I have decided to separate the way of explaining the exercises so that it is understood, but, really, everything flows in the moment.

You do not have to have only one way of doing things. The important thing is that the exercise is understood, and the nuances focused on the objective of the task as well.

If they understand it just by explaining it to them, great; If you have to show it to them so that they see it and imitate it, this is also valid. Your perception, the age of the players and how complex the exercise is also has an influence on, how much you have to intervene during the explanation.

Ask questions

This is something that I use a lot in training or consolidation of knowledge of my players. I perform tasks that require decision-making at some point in the exercise or at many points during the exercise.

When I explain the task, I ask questions that allow them to reflect on the other options they have in different situations. **This is a way to keep them thinking during training, not to be distracted and to consolidate concepts**. In addition, I receive information on what they understand or what they have learned during the session.

Even when you do an analytical exercise, it is good to incorporate a decision-making element because it is more productive and fun for them.

Tone of voice and confidence

Each coach has their own personality and their way of getting the information across to the players. However, once you are well-positioned on the field, you should use a voice loud enough so that they can hear you without shouting. Of course, you must master the topic you are going to explain so that you always demonstrate confidence.

In my early days as a coach, I made a lot of mistakes. I learned that even if you are not 100% certain about a topic, if you use the right tone of voice and display confidence, they will usually believe what you are saying. If you doubt yourself, they will doubt you. The embarrassment of public speaking is corrected with practice.

Execution speed in technical actions

Teaching the technique to your players is really not that difficult, they must imitate a body position and with practice they improve it. Although not all of them understand the importance of performing **technical actions with speed.**

If we compare elite football with amateur football, one of the main differences is the speed of the game together with the technical precision.

TRAIN TO COMPETE

The speed of the execution is an important aspect that you must take into account when explaining and performing the exercises. We will talk about this in the next topic.

Making corrections

Individual correction

If during the first actions of the task, the majority understood what they should do, but some players found it difficult to understand, you can let the exercise continue and approach those who are having difficulty so you can help them.

It is normal that players make mistakes, even if they understand what they have to do, either in their technical execution or in their decision-making. **In some cases, we should not stop the drill to correct just one player, it is better that the exercise continues and to correct them separately**.

It is important to separate the player from the group for individual correction, because most do not like to be corrected in front of others, both children and adults alike. Also, you must let them experiment, make mistakes, and not saturate them with corrections.

Many coaches scold players when they make a technical mistake or miss a goal in a game. That is wrong. **We must understand that they always do their best, and that there is an opponent who is trying to make things difficult**. The processes take time and sometimes we want to be coaches who solve everything in one day. Teach them, don't penalize them. ·

In addition, you will have players who have internalized wrong movement patterns with many years of practice. In that case, it takes time to modify that pattern or even, sometimes, it is not worth correcting the movements if it contributes positive things to the team or if it does not harm them.

Group corrections

These are usually done when the group did not understand the explanation well, or when the exercise is more complex than your players are able to do; It also works to clarify certain nuances.

To correct, you can stop the task, explain it again and see the results. If you see that it still does not work, you must modify or introduce a variant that facilitates the exercise to meet the objectives.

I have focused on the individual and group corrections in the exercises. But you can also correct attitudes, player behaviours, etc. There will be days when, during an exercise, they are not attentive or are distracted. That is when you can also correct behaviours.

Feedback

During the tasks you, must give reinforcements. Feedback is nothing more than an opinion about one or more people during an activity to evaluate their performance. **Those messages must be positive and can work both to congratulate and to correct**. When you tell the players what they are doing well, they will understand that this is the right way, and they will try to maintain it.

There is a widely used strategy in education to correct something in people; **this is called the sandwich technique**. It consists of saying something to the player that they have done well (positive), then you tell them what to correct (intelligently and not negatively) and end by saying something positive about their action.

TRAIN TO COMPETE

Example: if your player dribbles and then passes, but does not use the technique you have taught them, you could say:

"Luis, I see that you have improved your dribbling, you are doing very well"; "I want you to now be sure to make passes with the inside of your foot"; "Maintain that same power, you are doing excellently well."

In short: positive reinforcement + what you want to correct (what and how to do it) + positive reinforcement.

At the end of the session, you can ask questions to see if the concepts explained during the session have been understood. It is useless to feel that the training was successful if they do not know what they did or why they did it. **If you want to be a good coach and compete, you must focus on your players learning something, understanding it and being able to apply it in games**.

CHAPTER III

HOW TO DEVELOP YOUR TEAM FASTER

THE KEY POINTS

Taking into consideration the conditions of your team, the context in which you play and the individual preparation that each player can offer you, it is equally necessary to know how to develop and evolve the collective capacity of your team.

This chapter will cover the most important aspects needed to achieve growth in your team.

INTRODUCTION

Football is simple. To win, we must score one more goal than the opposition, it's easy, right? Everyone has an opinion on what is wrong with their favourite team, what needs to be improved, the transfers, the formations, etc. But do they really understand the whole context? In most cases, no. They are mere fanatics.

The same thing happens to us, many times we act as fanatical coaches, but not practical ones. **We believe that we know a lot when sometimes we know very little about the important details**.

I remember the phrase I read from Johan Cruyff: "Every trainer talks about movement, about running a lot. I say don't run so much. Football is a game you play with your brain. You have to be in the right place at the right moment, not too early, not too late…" [1].

---

1 See *https://www.marca.com/futbol/barcelona/2016/03/24/ 5691291246163f46068b45ef.html*

TRAIN TO COMPETE

In a match, we usually ask our players to run and move, but they don't understand where or why. Often, they do not know what to do because we do not understand it ourselves to be able to teach it to them.

You can win, simply by being better than the opposition, but when you lose, it is usually the only time you question yourself. At that moment you think that something is missing, you feel that the players seem not to be developing as you expected; the exercises are not being so productive or, at least, you get to the game, and you do not perceive that development.

I ask: are you doing the exercises based on **match-like situations**, with similar circumstances (relative time, space, and rhythm)?

There is no single science for football. Nobody has a magic wand that they can wave to make a player develop to a certain level or have certain knowledge. But all coaches agree that practice helps you improve, and that, normally, the more you perform an action, the better you will perform it. That is to say, if a player performs many repetitions of passes with the inside of the foot every day in training sessions, this will improve their passing, right? Everything indicates that this is the case.

But does this mean that that player is always going to pass well in a match because they have perfected their technique? The answer is NO. That player will be improving their technique without match-like stimulation, and in a match, there are many factors that have an effect: the opponent marking them, the time and space they have to give that pass, the positioning of their teammate they are passing the ball to, the positioning of the opponent, if the ball is in motion, bouncing, etc.

So, if a player receives many hours of technical skills training, they will develop based on the context in which they perform the action.

Nor am I saying that if you do the opposite, the player will always be effective in games; no. There are many influencing factors, but the closer the training is to what the player will experience in the game, the more tools they will have to respond efficiently to the stimuli of the game.

So, many players develop faster with weekend experience than with practice in training. If we do not extrapolate the training with what happens in a football game, the players can develop those actions that they carry out by adding hours of training, but they will not respond in the same way to situations with different stimuli.

Here are some ideas that can help you train and empower your team for competition.

STRATEGIES

Execution speed

Football in 2020 is different from football in 2000 and will continue to evolve. Counteracting defensive tactics requires not only good decision making and technical precision, but also execution speed.

In a match, the time and space a player has with the ball, or a possible recipient, is decisive. In certain positions or circumstances of the game there will be those who have to make decisions in a limited time that also benefit from the speed at which the previous action is carried out.

Most trainers have worked on the technique, thinking that our players were learning it from scratch. We usually do control exercises, dribbling, shooting, combined actions, passing wheels, possession, position games, mini games, etc., without asking for speed in the execution.

By this I do not mean that all football plays should be based on speed alone. Often, we must break up the game, either to slow down, to move the opponent and generate space, to capture the attention of an opposing player, to wait for teammates' movements, among others.

However, teaching technical gestures and actions with speed **is going to be similar to how quickly they have to perform many actions in a match**.

Rhythm of training

The rhythm of a match can vary depending on the tactical approach, the play style of each team or the actions that are carried out. But, in training, that rhythm has to be set by the coach. That is, **there needs to be continuity in the exercises, avoiding unnecessary breaks**, especially if we have two hours of training a week.

For example, if you have several balls, do not do drills with long lines of players, since the time it takes for everyone to do that activity generates fewer technical executions.

Choose exercises where you have the most players moving, or failing that, make sure the time it takes to start between one and the next is short. Reps are important for improvement, but don't forget about recovery.

If you have 60 minutes of training you should take advantage of it taking into account the physical load of the week, recovery time, exercise requirements, the age of your players, etc. If you want your players to develop faster, there has to be a rhythm to the training, so **they do enough repetitions to help them improve.**

Demand attitude

Many coaches call everything that happens in football '**intensity**': running, jumping, striking the ball, defending, attacking; even winning or losing. They say: "we won because we played with intensity", "we lost because we were not intense enough". **But how can we measure intensity in these types of actions or circumstances?** It is a term that is used often and that for me does not say anything about what happens in a match.

Barcelona lost 4-0 at Anfield vs. Liverpool in the Champions League (2019), being eliminated after winning 3-0 at Camp Nou. Was it a lack of intensity? I wouldn't say that Barça didn't play at 100% intensity in every action, but there were lapses in concentration, errors caused by the opponent and circumstances that they could not solve. This is football.

However, if you want to convey it as intensity because that is the way your players understand it, great. The idea is that the message gets through, and if your players respond well to that message, keep it up.

I will call everything you have to ask of your players in training and games 'attitude'. Attitude means the behaviour that a person has before certain actions. In football we would focus on commitment, conviction, responsibility, etc.

If a player loses the ball, they must be committed to trying to get it back as soon as possible. If a goal is scored, the players cannot let their heads go down (surrender) but keep trying until the end of the match.

So, in each training exercise, your team must give the maximum, that will improve both individual and collective performance in the game. **You might win and you might lose, but attitude is non-negotiable.**

Choose situations they can experience

During 90 minutes of play there are many different stimuli that your players must react to. We cannot control everything because the same action is presented in different ways, be it due to the speed of the ball, the terrain, the opponent's movements, the body position, etc.

TRAIN TO COMPETE

But planning training sessions with situations similar to the weekend will make the players and the team develop faster. For this, the vast majority of exercises must be done with opponents who condition decision-making **based on a tactical structure or real situations.**

What exercises simulating match situations can you do? Many. The truth is that you just need a little creativity and to think about how the situations in the game are given by position or lines. For example:

1v1 (forward vs goalkeeper), 1v1 (attacker vs defender), 2v1, 2v2, 3v2, 3v3, etc., ending with a shot on goal or mini goal:

These types of situations are common for making offensive and defensive decisions with different man-advantages or with equal players. Counter-attacking actions are usually simulated in a match and working defensively: coverage, swaps, defensive profile, marking, anticipation, interception, retreat. Offensively: unchecking, support, passes with decision-making, transitions, among others.

Combined actions

These are technical actions between 2 or more players with or without opposition. I usually use it with finishing on goal since the player, after performing a series of technical actions, competes to score more goals. Focus on your goal and add obstacles that they can experience.

Often, I perform combined actions without opposition so that they perform many repetitions of the technical gesture, without having to think so much. If you include opposition, it will be more real, but you must bear in mind that it can slow down the exercise.

Possession

If you want to work on technical aspects with decision making, this is a good resource so that they have to experience "similarities" to match situations. Although, I am not really in favour of making possession a priority for certain ages without tactical structure.

In general, I would use it as a warm-up or playful strategy. Because, if they master the basic technical aspects, I focus more on the technical-tactical rather than the merely technical. Possession does not usually have tactical content; therefore, it is not the most real thing that a player is going to experience on the weekend.

Mini matches

These are ideal for working on decision-making, tactics, technique, etc. Small groups of players participate, with equality or numerical superiority. Being relatively small spaces, interaction with the ball and decision-making are constant.

Position games

These are about generating superiorities from the position of your players. This is the key to working on tactics together with decision-making, associated with the position that your players are going to fulfil in the game.

Depending on the age, this may be more or less important. If they are children, I don't think they have to work on a specific position. In that case, you must rotate them so that they experience various positions. **If they are teenagers or adults, should train preferably by position because that's what they will do when they compete**.

It's what I enjoy doing the most with my players, with the combinatorial style. Starting from the following premise: "Nobody gives a pass for the sake of it. The passes have a purpose: to eliminate opponents. And if this is not possible, the players keep the ball or dribble seeking to attract opponents".

TRAIN TO COMPETE

Here is a very interesting web page for you to read a little more about the position game.[2]

Starting an attack from the goalkeeper

If you want to combine everything, you will have to train the beginning of the game with the goalkeeper and the different presses they can put on you. What will your players do if at the start you have 1 opponent, 2 or 3? Where should the free players be positioned according to each situation that the opponent may present? When should they offer support and when should they not? Etc. You should, according to your style, raise these situations in training and explain the possible options.

If you play a direct attacking style, you must also consider other factors. There will be more details in the following offensive and defensive play style topics. But, if you want them to improve, **they must know what to do in each game situation according to their position, opponent, and style of play**.

Your players must understand what they are doing and have the ability to execute it

To achieve success during training, the player **must understand what they are doing.** But that goes together with having a team with the technical and cognitive capacity to be able to perform the exercises you propose.

---

2   See at *https://www.martiperarnau.com/el-juego-de-posicion/*

CHAPTER IV

OFFENSIVE GAME STYLES: ACCORDING TO PLAYER CHARACTERISTICS AND EXTERNAL FACTORS

HOW TO BOOST YOUR TEAM OFFENSIVELY

Attacking in football is fundamental. The good condition of a player in a match is built up of many aspects. For example, the control of the ball with the goalkeeper, the decisive capacity of a player in a 1v1 duel, the audacity of the player in the face of pressure from the opponent, the circumstances of the game, etc. There are certain factors that condition the performance of the players.

This chapter provides a general overview of what these aspects are and what strategies are recommended to deal with this from a strictly offensive point of view.

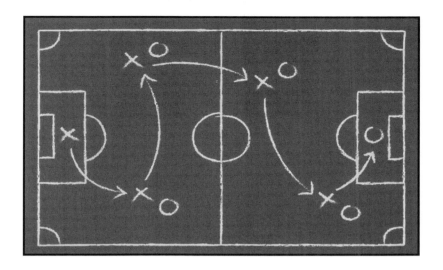

INTRODUCTION

You already have your team, and you know the characteristics of your players; now, it's up to you to develop the style you are going to use to attack and defend. You will often not know where to start and what aspects to take into account to know if you play combinative or if you play direct; some things are just common sense. However, the logical often goes unnoticed.

It is important to clarify that the style of play does not have to follow a unique structure. Sometimes we develop a style that we have to modify shortly afterwards because we feel it is not the right one or because of a poor run in matches, and the players do not believe in what is being done. Do not worry if things do not work out as you expected, **experience will help you avoid some mistakes, but other factors are out of your control**.

To choose a play style you must take into account: what your idea of football is, the characteristics of your players, the dimensions of the field, the condition of the grass, the mentality of the club, the style they previously had, the fans (in some cases) and even in some situations what the players feel and believe. I am speaking to you about various levels and teams. The common thing is to find a club where a specific style is not required from you, so you can choose.

As a coach, it is normal to have one style that we like more than another. Although sometimes **we must adapt to the conditions we have in a club or look for another option** (another team where you can try to use it). In amateur football, we are going to find dirt pitches, small and even in poor condition. If you like the combinatorial style of play, sometimes these fields are not ideal to implement it.

I will discuss some ideas that can help you decide on an offensive style of play when you arrive at a team, taking into account the characteristics of your players and external factors. I will add specific defensive ideas to complement the points.

STRATEGIES

Combinatorial attack style

The combinatorial attack, briefly defined, is to attract opponents to find free men and keep progressing in the game. Therefore, technical mastery you're your players' understanding of the game is important.

To better understand the combinatorial attack, I recommend that you read the position game article that I discussed in the previous topic to understand that everything has a why and a what for.

If you arrive at a club and want to do a combined style of play native, you should take into account:

A goalkeeper who dominates the game with his feet

Recently football has evolved a lot and goalkeepers who do not have a good command of the ball with their feet find it difficult to find a clear exit when they are under pressure. You don't have to be an expert, but you do have to master the basics.

The technical level of your players, especially in defence (centre backs):

If you cannot start a clean play from the back (beating opponents with control and passing), you cannot play combinatorial. Since, under pressure from the opponent, your team will not be able to progress from the goal kick, losing the ball in dangerous areas.

The midfield line with control of the ball and understanding of the game

It is ideal is to have at least one midfielder who knows how to offer good support to get out of pressure, progress with oriented control and have efficient decision-making skills. In this way, everything good that your defensive line does will benefit from the participation or movement of this player.

Speed in the offensive zone

This is not mandatory, but it helps a lot. A combinatory team, if it does not have speed up top, facilitates the pressure from the opposition. When the minutes tick by where they have you locked up in your half, if you do not have the option of speed behind the defenders, it is difficult for you to play out certain plays, unless the precision of your players' passes, and movements are very good. Therefore, having some speed can benefit you if they mark the man looking to play behind their defenders.

Good 1v1 from your attackers

This style allows you to progress through the game without having to dribble in dangerous areas. If done well, you can find players in attacking zones (forwards or wingers) with a 1v1 option with the defender.

If your attackers do not have a good level of dribbling, speed and/ or feints, your team must be very precise with the previous actions, thus reaching advantageous situations when they pressure you in your half, or even when they retreat.

Daring players (decision-making)

Playing combinative you run a certain risk in defensive and offensive zones with passes or movements.

You must teach your players what to do in match circumstances, but they too must have the ability to dare and resolve situations.

When you are pressured in your half, in some circumstances, things don't go the way we train them. Each opponent offers a different situation, and no matter how much you train them, your players must solve and make more complex decisions based on what they perceive in seconds.

Variants

Rivals are going to present you with different defensive situations in matches. It is becoming increasingly difficult to counteract the defensive approaches of well-trained teams.

If your team is not very precise and they pressure you up the field with many players, **there will be a greater chance of turnover in your half, which could create a possible scoring chance for your opponent**.

In these situations, you should alternate, from time to time, with direct attacks. This allows that in the following actions the opposition team does not know if it should pressure you with the same number of players or with fewer, that is when you can go out playing combinative again.

On possible loss of possession

The combinatorial style of play leaves the team at a large and disadvantageous situation if the opposing team manages to recover the ball in a certain sector, especially at the start.

You will possibly have fewer players to defend transitions and in bad settings.

To master it, a lot of training is required in the basic principles of position play, kicking the ball, understanding the game, finding a free man, etc. But they must not only learn to combine, **also to foresee a potential loss depending on the circumstances**. The players further away can be interpreting the fluidity of the play to come closer and give support or stay wide.

Once your players understand it, assimilate it and master it, you will know that it is not as risky as it seems, but it is not enough just that the players know it, they must practice it every week.

Do not expect immediate results. Do not expect the team to play combinative from the beginning and to perfection; it is a process that takes time.

Direct attacking style

This is a style widely used in most amateur teams, although many without criteria or purpose. There are many coaches who assure that

TRAIN TO COMPETE

their team plays "combinatorial" because they pass one or two passes on the defensive line and then progress to direct play. That is not combinatorial, that is a direct attack.

The intention of the direct attack is to reach the rival goal with the fewest possible passes.

On the other hand, it is one thing to strike without purpose and another to have a direct attacking style. **If your players don't know where they are hitting the ball, when and why; then you are not training this way of attacking**, you are simply playing hoofball.

The direct attack style can be considered as a way of dividing the ball. And, in a way, it can be that you are hitting it so that there is a 50/50 and then a second play that can fall to you or it can fall to the opponent. But within dividing the ball, there must be logical criteria to try to tip the balance to your side.

- It is advisable to have a goalkeeper who can **strike the ball well and has precision with long passes**. If you don't have that player, you should at least have a centre-back who can make that initial long ball. If your goalkeeper or centre backs do not have good distribution, ask yourself: where are they going to hit successfully and who is going to do it? If you have other players who can do it, you should evaluate if it is worth changing their position constantly during the game.

- You must have offensive players with height or at least **good at covering and/or contesting the ball to win in direct play and have chances of a successful attack**. This is common sense. If you want to win the aerial balls, you must have players with good potential for jumping and heading or covering the ball. But this is not the only method.

- If you are pressured upfield and your attacking players are not taller than the opponent, you can propose a different direct attack. For example, hitting the ball from the defensive line at mid-height so that the recipient can play face-to-face with a teammate without having to jump with the opponent.

- It is not only important who is going to compete for the ball, but the subsequent action so as not to lose it (second ball). When a player receives a ball with his back to the opponent's goal, they must have close options to support them (**well-positioned teammates**), or a lot of technical quality to be able to get out of the pressure and continue to progress.

- Also, you can alternate with an unmarked support (attracting the opponent) and a player who moves into the space that their partner left and hit that sector after moving the opposition markers. Or even accumulate more players in a sector and even if you know that you may lose the first ball, you will also have a greater chance of winning the second ball. These are just a few ideas; you must think more about them according to the characteristics of your players.

- If you have a player with good physical potential to play aerial balls, in the game, put him against an opposition defender who you think they can beat and not against one of the same size or who has defensive qualities. It is a small nuance that helps a lot.

The better you control these situations, **the probability of winning that second ball is increased very much** compared to just playing long balls for the sake of it.

If you play on a small pitch

It is common to find pitches of minimum or similar dimensions to be able to play. Now, what do we normally see in this situation? Logically, there will be more 1v1 duels, ball disputes, shots, crosses into the area and set pieces (throw-ins, fouls far from the area, corner, etc.) due to a higher probability of contact as there is less time and space to decide.

Can you play combinatorial on small pitches? Of course you can. This is an option, but you should know that the things most likely to occur on these fields are the actions mentioned above.

Therefore, to play combinative in this situation, you need greater precision and speed of execution from your players, since the opponent has to travel fewer metres, compared to a large field, to try to steal the ball.

I have played on small fields with a combined style of play with youth teams (because it is my favourite style; and, in these circumstances, I had players with the qualities to do that), but I have had to alternate the short game with the long game many times because of rival pressure.

Sure, my players understood what to do in many circumstances. When they came to pressure us with 4 or 5 players, we looked for space with a direct play because in attack they let us duel 1v1 and we were also good at those, that caused them to doubt what to do in the following actions. We got promoted that season.

Additional considerations

- On small pitches, the wings do not tend to reach attacking areas very often. You will seldom see a wing back send the ball down the wing because **the time and space of the receiving player is short**. For this reason, it is difficult for the winger to have time to reach attacking positions without the winger having made a decision conditioned by the opponent, except in plays that start from higher up the pitch like a throw-in or free kick.

- In the defensive phase, you must bear in mind that, as it is a small field, there will be many long balls. The referee will have difficulty perceiving all possible offsides, because there can be many actions and some to the limit. If you avoid playing offside, the better.

Starting from that idea, in the offensive phase you can take advantage of that circumstance. As the referee is going to find it difficult to blow all offside decisions, alternating the short game with the long game, looking for spaces, can sometimes generate 1v1s against the goalkeeper.

- Regarding set pieces, it is logical that the throw-ins will be given more times than in a large field. If you have a player who can throw the ball from near the rival area to put the ball around the penalty spot, you can train them to take advantage. **The most goals that are scored on a small field come from a set-piece (throw-in, corner kick, fouls and even goal kick).**

You must also teach how to defend these actions, because you will find many opponents who have a good throw-in or free kick. Even distant midfield fouls can also be dangerous if they hit the ball into the area (it is common for them to do so). You must train them both in attack and defence.

- Half of the games of the season are played at home, the other half will be played on small, normal, or large fields. **It would be ideal to structure a team that is strong on your field** and that adapts outside of it.

- If you can't choose players, **you must generate a style of play that allows you to empower your team**.

Counterattacking style

Like the direct attack, this is about reaching the opposing goal as soon as possible. However, the counterattack seeks, after recovering the ball, to surprise the opponent who is defensively disorganized. It is interesting and widely used today.

The idea is, after recovering the ball, with the least number of passes possible, to put yourself in a shooting position at the rival goal.

For this, **we must consider recovery situations of the ball in different areas of the field**, with movements of offensive zones according to circumstances and situations that the rival may present, to take advantage of those spaces that they leave in the defensive disorganization.

CHAPTER V

DEFENSIVE GAME STYLES: ACCORDING TO PLAYERS CHARATERISTICS

HOW TO BOOST YOUR TEAM DEFENSIVELY

In the previous chapter we talked about the ability of players to develop their full potential when attacking. In football, attacking is decisive, but it must be accompanied by a good defensive structure.

Considering the players' marking, their speed, the reading of the game and their concentration are also aspects to be highlighted. This section assesses how a footballer should respond when the team is defending during a match.

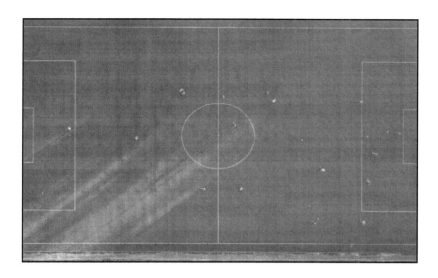

STRATEGIES

Although I have already explained some defensive ideas, at this point I will only talk about the defensive phases and how to take advantage:

The press

All coaches know what it means to push. However, when should you do it? Should it always be done? Does the opponent have an influence? Everything is subject to change.

You can press from the outset of the rival play, a ¾ press, a half-court press, after losing the ball, at a throw-in, etc. The characteristics of your players and, of course, the opponent have an influence.

It is not the same to press a team that plays the direct attack very well in the opposite half than to do it with one who plays combinative and does not dominate the game for long periods. **There is no one way to do things, because even doing what seems logical, you can lose**

Height of your defensive line

If your defensive players are short in stature compared to rivals, you must foresee that, by pressing, you might be on the receiving end of long balls from your opponent and that, possibly, they will beat you in the air.

It's hard to specify which action is correct in these cases, but bear in mind that, if you go with your whole team up, they will strike. Once they send the ball high, the first action is possibly won by their height advantage and your team must be very attentive to the second ball.

One option: let the opponent play out from the goal kick and wait for them with the team together and then press in specific areas.

Another option: press with some players and the rest waiting behind, making it more likely that the first 50/50 is contested by the midfield line and not the defensive one.

It will depend on the characteristics of your players and the strengths/weaknesses of the rival.

One common mistake is to push teams that have a good direct attack too high. But if your players are taller in stature than your opponents, maybe you should go to pressure and try to win in duels.

If your defence is slow

If you do not have fast players who provide balance in defence, if you press high, your team must be aware of balls behind the defensive line. **I would recommend teaching your players to always take steps**

back when the opponent is going to feint the shot. Also, knowing that they are slow, try to always be one metre behind their attackers.

If you press high with a slow defence and the opponent plays balls behind the centre backs, it could lead to a one on one with your goalkeeper because there will not be enough time for help to arrive. Who comes out to pressure and who takes steps back should be coordinated very well to avoid being beaten in those situations.

If you are better than your opponent 1vs1

If your team is very good in duels and you outperform your rival in that regard, it may be a good idea to go and put pressure on in the rival half; and even put pressure on the man so that they cannot combine comfortably and have to constantly move the ball.

Retreat

This is another defensive tactic that can be used at various times in the game. Like pressing, you have to take into account the characteristics of the opponent and those of your team.

Your players must be clear on when and to which area of the pitch to retreat to. It can be done in ¾ of the pitch, halfway or in your own half (widely used today).

Once you are beaten after a spell of pressure, **it is recommended to retreat to bring the team together in some area of the field, preventing the rival from getting any further.**

At this point, as with the press, it is very complex to define everything you have to take into account. However, I will mention when you could use the retreat in specific situations:

If your opponent is much superior to your team

Firstly, we must define: Far superior in what? With the control of the ball? In direct play? In aerial duels? In 1vs1? From there you must evaluate where and how you will retreat if you deem it appropriate or have a trained pattern according to circumstances.

Let's imagine that due to the difference in level, they are winning many phases of the game: the most common in this case is to make an intense retreat (in your own half), since going to pressure the ball in their half can be suicide.

It is common sense and much better, if you are going to be beaten in all areas and phases, to have the team together, close to your goalkeeper, and from there defend so that they cannot probe comfortably. The less space they have to attack, in theory, the more difficult it will be to break down your lines.

You must bear in mind that, in that case, you will be defending most of the time with your team together. That will mean you have little time on the ball and that the opponent occupies almost all the sectors of your half.

To attack, you can propose possible counterattack situations, since if you try to combine once the ball has been recovered in intense retreat (with the opposition team in your half), you may lose it as a result of the opponent's location and pressure.

When they beat your team lines with a pass

Depending on the location on the pitch, once they pass a team line in one sector, their progression can soon become dangerous. **Your players, or at least some of them, should retreat**. I know it seems logical, but many times when they get past your midfield, the defensive line keeps coming out to press, leaving a dangerous space behind.

In this case, instead of pressing, the defenders must retreat (move back) and must not go out unless they have numerical superiority to counter the attack quickly or it is a very clear action with a defensive advantage, or they are close to their own area. The idea of retreating is to slow down the rhythm of the rival attack to allow time for help from your team to arrive, thus avoiding being beaten.

If your defence is slow

I previously commented that if you have slow players in your defensive line, you should take into consideration that balls in behind can do a lot of damage when you go to press. On the other hand, retreating and waiting for the opponent with a slow defence **can be a good strategy to prevent balls from getting played in behind your defenders**. And, if they play them while your defence are sat back, it has to be a very precise ball because there will be less distance between the defence and the goalkeeper.

I don't mean that you should only retreat if you have a slow defensive line. This is only an alternative. It depends on the characteristics of your players, on how the opponent plays and on other factors such as the dimensions of the field, pitch condition, etc.

When the team is tired or you have to look after a lead/protect a draw

There are phases of the game where physical exhaustion starts to become noticeable, either through pressing many times, because your team is not match-fit, because of the opponent's style vs. yours, and even to protect a lead or play out a draw.

If your opponent begins to have control of the ball and creates some sense of danger, your team will surely end up making intensive retreats.

It is better to retreat and stick together to press in your own half than to press high ineffectively out of exhaustion, giving space for the rival attack. So, this must be trained.

Retreat does not mean that you should not press

That means **you retreat because the opponent or the phase of the match is forcing you to.** But the subsequent intention is to press where you think it will be easier to steal the ball back or where there is less danger.

If you are going to retreat in your own half (intense retreat), you must teach your players when and how to press to lock your opponent in some area of the field and be able to recover the ball. Maybe you should go to press when the ball goes to the opposition's wing back, when the ball is played inside, or when the ball goes out wide and the wingers have help nearby. Then it is what you decide based on what the opponent does, their characteristics and yours.

Pressing or retreating depends on many factors and moments of the match. There are teams that prefer to play this way all the time because their greatest virtue is to attack on the counter. Therefore, they tend to give up possession of the ball to the rival and wait for them, even if they are losing.

Analyse what is best for you for your team, for the level of the league, your pitch and train it. **It is not enough just to tell your players what to do.**

CHAPTER VI

READY TO COMPETE

Our journey so far has been through classes, instructions, and strategies that every coach must have in their arsenal. Now, these teachings must bear fruit in a match.

This chapter attempts to review everything that can happen in a game after you have trained with your players.

INTRODUCTION

This section is designed especially for coaching players over 14 years of age (including adults), because there tend to be different nuances and objectives than in beginners grassroots football. Of course, the more adults there are, the greater the complexity of the training sessions.

I believe that from 14 years old you can start to be competitive, depending on the club, its objectives, etc. **The ages of 14, 15, 16 years are still formative stages in certain aspects**, but most of these players are already ready to undergo training focused on the competition, because they have a greater capacity to understand the game and better physical development.

Also, at 14 years and older, they usually know which position they are best in, alternative positions or even their strengths that lead them to develop in one area of the field more than another, although this may vary.

TRAIN TO COMPETE

There are cases where professional players modify their position after competing at an elite level for many years: Jesús Navas from winger to wing back, Sergio Ramos from wing back to centre-back, Bale from wing back to winger, Buffon from striker to goalkeeper, Mascherano from midfielder to centre-back, among others.

If they give you a team with the ideal age and characteristics to start being competitive, what should you take into account? First, include tactical exercises and understanding of the game in conjunction with physical and technical capacities.

Remember that for most teams you work on, the goal of the players is to do exercise and enjoy football, so I know this chapter can divide coaches' opinion due to the age involved.

My intention is not to debate what the ideal age is to be competitive, but to give you the tools so that you can structure the training sessions, taking into account the positions of certain players and working on your game model in a short time.

I'm going to give you 12 ideas that will help you to be competitive, supposing that you start with a team and train two days a week, or maybe three. I will briefly repeat some of the information presented in this book to give structure to the strategies, but I will only delve into the relevant information.

This does not mean that this is the only or the best way to competitive. Each coach can develop their training or match ideas according to their global vision of football.

STRATEGIES

Observe the characteristics of your players

The first thing you have to do when they give you your team is to observe what characteristics your players have in terms of size (height), physique (build), technical mastery, speed, ball movement, decision-making, etc.

Normally we start a pre-season with the team, and we usually plan training with physical or technical circuits. The problem is that we might not know our players and those exercises give us little information.

So, **the first thing we have to do is put them in a game and "watch and learn"**. I think you get the idea, it's not that watching. You must write down what you consider important about your players to build the team's game model.

Plan games with reduced numbers, mini-matches or matches with shorter game time than normal and a lot of recovery time (because, surely, they have had several weeks without training). If you don't know what you have, what type of training are you going to do and how do you intend to play?

Forget about physical pre-season and isolated physical sessions

How many times have we structured training sessions working on physical, technical and tactical conditions in isolation? For many years that has been the ABC of football, and it is still done in many places.

Vítor Frade dedicated himself to understanding that these separate concepts did not make sense when related to in-game transference, because all these aspects happened at once. So, he developed a work methodology called "Tactical Periodization", **where in the exercise all the existing aspects of the football match are globalized**.

You can read the book "What is tactical periodization?" by Xavier Tamarit with Vítor Frade. If you are starting out in the world of coaching, it will be a little complex, but it will give you very interesting insights for your training and the conception of current football.

That does not mean that training using this methodology is the only way to train or that it is the best, but I do want you to reflect on something:

You have to train a team 2 or 3 days a week, you should have 60 minutes of training and hopefully you have 90. Are you going to spend that little time working physical fitness? Remember that you have to train your players at a tactical level to be competitive in a soccer match.

Why not incorporate the physical aspect with the ball where you work on tactical aspects and the play style you are going to use?

I know this idea may seem a bit complex, when I was first learning it was difficult for me to internalize it because I was used to other strategies, but it can be done. You should think about what exercises you can do, incorporating tactics with the physical and the technical. Position games are a great example of this.

Choose a play style

Once we have identified the characteristics of the players, we must choose a style of play that adapts and enhances the team we have. **It is true that every style can be put into practice with any team, but there are some that are better adapted to certain players.**

Maybe you want to start a combinatorial attack out from the back to attract the opponent and then move past lines with passes or win the ball further forward with 1v1 duels.

Or you can just hit from the goal kick by accumulating players in an area and hope to win the second ball.

You could even combine the styles (this is ideal) so that, when your players face opponents who withdraw or press, they have the tools to overcome these circumstances. Apply what you think is best with the players you have.

But you should not only improve in attack, also in how you defend. Know if your team is good at 1v1 duels to press your opponent high up the pitch or not. It is also advisable to know if your central defenders are fast or slow to move the line up or to retreat back. All this has an influence.

I have already talked about styles. Analyse your team and decide what suits you best depending on their qualities.

Train match situations

We have mentioned it before, if your team trains based on what is going to be achieved in a competitive match, it will be easier for them to be successful in their actions. So, if you have 2-3 days of training a week, **focus on introducing the players to game situations.**

Teach them how to attack, how to get out of a high press with 1 striker, with 2 or with 3, which area of the field to aim for and why, how to find free players, how your players should be positioned, how to defend, where to press, when to retreat, etc.

Analytically working on certain aspects can help to consolidate concepts. Also, some exercises are fun for players, but doing them often will make them bored. This will not be like what they experience in the game. So, try to incorporate all aspects as much as you can.

Physical load, muscle overload and injuries

I want to clarify that I am not a physical trainer so I will not speak scientifically about what you should have in consideration. However, I have had experiences that allow me to consider balancing workloads, especially training 2 or 3 days a week.

You should read and inform yourself a little about how aerobic and anaerobic capacities work. It is essential to study which actions are carried out the most in a football match so that you have some idea of what to emphasise in the session.

If you analyse the actions that the players carry out in a game, you will know that continuous runs (jogs) of one hour are not similar to what a player will carry out in a match. If you want to work on your team's physique from a tactical point of view, at least take into account what type of physical form you should work on that is adapted to the game.

However, we can control certain things to avoid superficial injuries or overload:

Training pace

This is the easiest way to see if your players are fatigued or not. If they no longer apply the same pressure, or are inaccurate with the ball in simple situations or the attitude with and without the ball is no longer the same as at the beginning, it might be that the load has been high or they have not had time to recover. In this case, give them more recovery time or less exercise time per repetition. Even if it is almost the end of the training, it is worth considering whether to stop it completely.

Muscle pain

If one or some of your players have some muscular discomfort after some exercises or repetitions, they may be overloaded from previous training or the movements that this task requires are not adequate for their physical capacity.

It could be your responsibility or theirs, but you should lower the load and let those players stop training that day if you see fit.

Don't do speed exercises at the end of training

Speed exercises require a high contraction of the muscles and a maximum demand for a certain time. If at the end of training, after having already completed several exercises, you put a high demand on a muscle that experiences fatigue, it is prone to injury.

Look at the faces and body language of your players

Another way of perceiving if the exercise load is very high or too low, is by observing how your players are doing during their rest periods. If you see that many look tired, or put their hands on their hips, or on their knees, maybe you could introduce more recovery time or less time in the next repetition. And if, on the contrary, they are very relaxed, you could reduce recovery time, modify distances, add variants, etc.

With these tips I do not mean that you need to control the loads or the exact times. These are ideas oriented more to some strategies designed with common sense. But, when you are working alone and you do not have a clear notion of the load of the exercise you want to do, **you can perceive more aspects that allow you to increase or decrease demand, time, distances, modify tasks, etc.** In this simple way, you can prevent, to some extent, muscle injuries and overloads.

Managing games

The pre-game talk should be to remind your players of certain aspects that they should take into account but **avoid giving ideas that they have never practiced before**. Maybe you can include small nuances, either by the opponent you are facing or certain modifications, but you cannot change the whole style of play without having previously trained it. In other words, you can change it, and you can even be better off for it, but it will be because of the quality of your players and not because you have planned or trained it.

I delve into this in the following topic: "Planning and managing football games".

"Play the way you train"

We often hear the typical phrase of "train the way you play". That means that if you train hard, you can play hard; if you train at 50%, you will play at 50%.

As coaches we must not only focus on training well, but also on asking the players to dare to put into practice exactly what they do in training during the game.

Therefore, I have coined that the phrase for the coach is the reverse: "Play the way you train", so that you ask your players, in a match, to do the actions they have been training and not the opposite due to the nerves of the game.

It is true that a lot of emotions enter a game, sometimes winning or losing is a minor detail, and you must make decisions depending on the circumstances.

You can modify the way you attack or defend to counter or surprise your opponent. Of course, they are there to stop you, and you must adjust when you see fit. What you should not do, for example, is train and teach the combinatorial style of play every day but demand they play direct attack without knowing how. That is why I say "play how you train."

To be competitive, the first thing you should do is try to get your players to put into practice everything they train during week. If your players play something very different, because you let them, then there is no real transfer to the game and knowledge is not consolidated.

Match stimuli are very different from training stimuli; it takes practice to build trust and confidence in the team.

The training day after the game

This is a good day to talk with your players about everything that was done over the weekend. Learn their views on what was done well (what has been trained), what can be improved and some general feelings. **The team needs to know what they are doing well to serve as positive reinforcement**, and they need to improve to work on it.

Send or show videos to your players

If you like this type of stuff, you might be a little "geeky" like me and watch and analyse football videos. It may be a good idea to send analysis videos to your players so they can see what game plan you want to implement.

Most of the players on your team are not used to working tactically, no one has taught them and sometimes explaining it to them on a whiteboard is not the same as being seen with examples.

Also, if possible, you can record your team's matches, make cuts of plays in their respective positions to later **correct them and make them watch them**.

Keep track of your matches

When you start the days of the competition, make a record and a short summary of the matches. Analyse how your attack and defence were, what things to maintain, to correct, as well as to collect some data about the opponent.

In all competitions (except cups with a knock-out match format) you will play home and away, therefore, you will face the same team again. If you record how they played, their best players and their weaknesses, it will help you prepare for the second leg.

It is true that the opponent may have another style of play and different players after several weeks, but if you have written information about them, it will be easier to plan.

Analyse the opposition before playing

When you analyse your opponents you will be able to see how they attack and how they defend according to the circumstances. If we are in a grassroots or amateur football club, it is difficult to go and watch rival matches, but if you have the opportunity, it is an important point to be competitive.

Later we will talk about how to analyse opposing teams and what aspects you must take into account to gain an advantage.

They are no longer children, they must be treated differently

We tend to constantly give children indications of what to do in training. In addition, we can make a mistake in some explanations, and they may not realize it.

When we talk about teenagers or adults, we know that cognitive development changes. If you want to make the same jokes that you do with the little ones or the same exercises in training, you are going to bore them. If you do not show confidence in what you explain, they will notice.

You must treat them with respect. You should not lose your sense of humor (if you have one) but adapt it to their age. **If you do not know how to treat them, it is better to observe them, be respectful and serious while learning from them, rather than trying to be funny and not fitting in.**

If you want to compete at a better level, you must first earn the trust of the group so that they feel comfortable with you. If they don't believe in you, they will doubt what you say and will not be objective when they lose. If they trust you, even if you lose, the majority will continue to support you and believe in what you do.

CHAPTER VII

PLANNING AND MANAGING FOOTBALL MATCHES

A football game is not just about attacking and defending. The coach leads the players; gives instructions, guides them, listens to them and motivates them. Communication is essential for this sport and this chapter will discuss this topic further.

Some logical coaching strategies can lead players to improving their footballing ability. Planning during practice and getting these ideas across during a match are the focal points of this chapter.

Álvaro Gómez-Rey

INTRODUCTION

Planning for a match allows us to plan what we are going to say, seeks to understand how we are going to approach it in terms of objectives and avoid any kind of improvisation.

We have all given pre-match talks with these generic sayings: "you have to ask for the ball", "you have to constantly be on the move", "intensity in everything you do", "everyone give 100%", "we are going to be aggressive", "we must pass and move", "we are at home and here we can't lose", "we have to keep the ball and control the game", "give your all out there", and others of that style.

TRAIN TO COMPETE

Very well, I understand that this talk is focused on motivating and invigorating the team, that is valid. Now, let's look at a couple of examples that can be given in that game after the same talk, and our possible reaction:

You lost 0-2. Your team did not control the game. They passed the ball for fear of losing it as a result of rival pressure. The second balls were in your favour, but you did not generate clear chances. They had two set pieces that ended in a goal, and you lost.

End of the game: You were very upset, you complained they did not dominate enough of the possession from the start. You told them that they were not playing with intensity, that they were not moving enough around the pitch. You told them that you can't lose at home and that it looked like they were scared because they weren't asking for the ball.

You won 2-0. Your team couldn't play as they trained. They passed the ball around for fear of losing it. The opposition created several clear openings that did not end in a goal. The second balls benefited you and, although your team did not do much damage, you had two set pieces that ended in a goal and you won.

End of the match: You were happy. You congratulated everyone for their effort and great game. You felt that the message motivated them and that they played with intensity for each ball as they should. Even if they didn't do what they practiced, you were proud.

These are two examples of the many that I can give you. **The conclusion of many coaches is that it is only about winning, no matter how or what happened**.

Yes, we compete because we want to win, but the idea is that you develop as a coach, your team understands what they are doing and what you train is improved. If you control the factors of the game with criteria similar to how they train, you will have more chances of achieving victory than leaving it to chance.

When you don't win, it seems that everything that went wrong was to do with the players' intensity. But, at a football level: What happened on the field? Did your players know how they should play according to the opponent's set-up? Did they generate clear chances? How? What was the opponent doing and how did they counter it? Could you have done something to change what happened? Etc.

Be a practical coach as you are going to experience a lot of wins and losses as in the example above. **You can dominate a game and lose. You can be much inferior to the rival on the field and end up winning**. This is football, anything can happen. When a lower team starts winning, they can be more energized, organize themselves well in defence and complicate the game for any higher-level team.

Understanding this, I ask the following questions to reflect on: How do you deal with the result in front of your players? Should you only focus on the result? If you win, does it mean there was intensity and if you lose, there wasn't? What is the individual and collective goal of your team? Why didn't your team play the way you wanted them to? Could it be that the players do not know what they have to do or did the opposition stop them from doing it? Could it be that your words of encouragement had no relation to what they train? Does effort only count when you win? Will you not be to blame?

You ask them in the game to "dominate the ball and attack together". But, how? Where? When? Who is going to give them superiority and in what area? I have already said it many times: the opponent is there to stop you.

Your pre-match talk should be aimed at reinforcing what they have trained or what they can do. I'm not saying that the talk in the example

TRAIN TO COMPETE

I raised was wrong, I'm just saying that, as a coach, you should be practical in in-game situations, without demanding things they don't know, or giving your players confusing instructions.

Then the post-game talk should not focus on the end result. **If you don't give a talk at the end of the game, all the better** (I'll explain why later).

You might be thinking: what does all this have to do with the planning and managing of matches? It has a lot to do with it. In fact, this is the most important thing. Before planning a game, **you should think about what they have between-training, what they can do and what they are not prepared to do**. The less knowledge they have about something, the more likely they are to fail.

STRATEGIES

Planning matches and pre-match talks

Goals

Just like in training, the first thing you should be clear about is your team's goals in each game. Enjoying and learning is the key to youth soccer training. As they get older, there may be other goals, whether competitive or formative sports.

Pre-match talk

Each coach has their own personality and idea of how to give their talks. But each human group you work with is different; it is not the same speaking with adults as it is with children.

I will give you some recommendations that will serve as a guide:

- **Initial message:** say hello, see how they are, how they feel. Talk about the pitch or even some jokes to reduce the tension of the match.

- **Structure the bulk of the talk in a maximum of 3 points:** The idea is to remember the important aspects that they must know: "attack, defence and set pieces".

- **Attack:** How will you attack, direct play? Combinatory attack? Mixed?

- **Defence:** How will you defend? High, medium or low line? Where do you press and when?

- **Dead ball:** any strategy you have or qualify the way to defend them.

End with a short motivational message. It's not mandatory. Summarize the tactics.

Players are supposed to have trained during the week on how they are going to play, so there is no need to saturate them with new information. If they are children, the ideas should be focused on enjoying the game, highlighting efforts made, etc. If they are teenagers or adults, you can focus on the goals of the team, what they have trained, the opponent, etc., but don't forget that they also play football because they enjoy it. **A lot of tactics is boring.**

The talk should be short

There is no exact time to give a talk. Many factors have an influence: the age of the players, the level of competition, the time you have, among other things. But, generally speaking, it should be brief.

Try to do it in less than 8-10 min. That includes: initial greeting, tactical messages and motivational message.

TRAIN TO COMPETE

In addition, **the attention span of the players is short**. If they are children, even less so. There is no use saturating them with information before the game that they will not be able to retain.

Write your talk and study it

Having the talk prepared will make you improvise less with your players. If you write the talks and reread it several times; you will be more likely to express your emotions with the clear ideas of the game.

At first, the routine of writing it down and remembering everything may be a bit difficult for you, but then it will make it easier for you to lead the group.

Warm up

Prepare the warm-up. You will know what materials you need and what you have available, avoiding improvisation. You must foresee if you are going to have half a pitch, a ¼ pitch or just a small side to warm up on. Have a structured warm-up for each situation.

In my case, I usually repeat the warm-up during the season, so the players know it and I don't have to explain it every weekend in detail. Depending on the opponent, the pitch, or the weather, I change little things.

I will not make a structure of the warm-up because there is already a lot of information on that, and it is not the point of this book. What I can tell you is that I include stimulation, passing actions for the sensations of the players with the grass, joint mobility, position play, some action combined with finishing and some final exits (sprint).

Although, there is no one structure. You can add, remove, or modify things, it is to the taste of each coach, taking into account the age of the players, the physical space available and the objective you want to refresh with the warm-up.

Managing the matches

Each coach expresses emotions in different ways. It is normal to transmit more energy in some games since our emotional state can vary according to the circumstances. **What we should not do is lose our sanity; It is a *sine qua non* requirement to be aware of what we say and do,** maintaining respect with our players, with the opponent, the referee and even parents. Otherwise, you will lose credibility and the trust of many. Remember that you are the leader; everyone is watching you.

From experience I can tell you that the emotions of the matches often prevent us from thinking clearly. We focus so much on a specific action that we are not able to observe everything that happens around us.

Sometimes in football it only takes a small change to affect the momentum of the game. If you want to train and would also like to win matches, you must learn to observe everything that happens in the game while controlling emotions, in this way, you will be able to control certain situations and think about what benefits you the most with respect to your team and the opposition.

But what is the best way to manage a match? Like Diego Simeone? Like Zidane? Like Guardiola? It would be a complex topic to discuss. Each coach has their own personality. However, I will give you my recommendations that many coaches agree on after having analysed coaches from grassroots, semi-professional, and professional football:

You must be objective

If the opponent is far superior to your team, there is little you can do to change the dynamics of the game. You must be patient, encourage, focus on small goals and not demand things that you have not taught them.

Do not narrate the game

Your players should already know how they have to play: if short or long, when and why, position on the field, etc., they are supposed to have been training them. So, give positive messages and encouragement, but don't be telling them everything they have to do. Let them think, make decisions, and make mistakes; this is how you learn. Only correct nuances.

Do not shout

I understand that there are circumstances where you must raise your voice because the player is far away from you so that they can hear some nuance, but that does not mean that you should shout excessively. If you want to convey security and confidence, yelling is not the best way. Also, it looks very ugly from the outside.

Make corrections without causing offence or criticizing the mistake

If you have to correct something during a match, do it politely. Many coaches use terms such as "wake up, the game has already started", "hurry up" (Spain), "you couldn't hit a barn door".

All these terms are negative because **you are criticising the person, and you are not correcting the action.**

You must be precise in the action that the player took, and want them to correct it. For example: "I want you to focus on who you are marking so that when the ball goes to them, you are closer, and you can steal the ball." The player usually knows when they have done wrong; if you criticize them for a mistake what you are doing is demotivating them. **Offer solutions.**

Control your body language

Avoid continuous gestures of the arms and legs. To give a message to your players or to the referee it is not necessary to move your arms excessively, they will not see you nor will you transmit any positive message.

Recognize when you are wrong

You must learn to recognize when you make a mistake. No coach is perfect, we all make mistakes, and you will too. In many moments you will make unwise decisions during a match.

Acknowledging that you have made a mistake in some circumstances is the best way to learn and teach your players that we can all make mistakes, and there is no problem with doing so.

Also, if you made the mistake with a player at some point in time, you should apologize. That will strengthen your relationship with them.

Try not to blame external factors

The referee will make bad decisions and we cannot control that, but others we can. You must recognize the mistakes of the team as a group, or yours in the decision-making, and stop reproaching others, as far as possible, because you cannot work on that.

Yes, there will be days when the referee is decisive in the game; I am not denying that, they are just trying to prevent criticism of external factors from being recurrent. Focus on objectively analysing the match and the factors that can be corrected.

Post-match talk

A great recommendation is that, at the end of the game, give a short talk or no talk at all.

Players come off with the stress of the match; win, lose or draw. If they have won, they will not pay as much attention because they are happy and what they want is to celebrate. If they have lost, they leave the field upset, what you tell them can make them more upset or lead them to feeling guilty. Leave this talk for training during the week.

What you can do at the end of the match **in one or two minutes is to give encouragement if they are sad and congratulate them for the effort**. But do not delve into tactical aspects, or in things that were not done well. It is time for them to lower their heart rate and rest.

CHAPTER VIII

ANALYZING MATCHES OBJECTIVELY

Not all matches are the same. Your team may be in excellent physical condition and have trained very hard. However, there are elements that can affect what we can expect from a game. The pitch, the weather, the level of the opponent, the number of training sessions are all important.

Therefore, analyze objectively, a match can offer you alternatives such as being able to score points in a match or stimulate the players' spirits.

INTRODUCTION

Do we usually watch football matches as fans, always observing the player with the ball? Or analyzing the situations that occur simultaneously on the field?

Analyzing games helps us understand what is happening on the field and then correct phases of the game. We must forget about the typical "lack of intensity" talks and focus on the practical: correcting positional errors, the way of attacking and defending, observing free spaces, and so on.

When we analyze a match, **we must control the emotions to observe the details**. Analyzing is not difficult; the difficult thing is to stay focused during 90 minutes to make effective decisions. I will mention some ideas that allow you to analyze the rival and your own team to take advantage.

TRAIN TO COMPETE

STRATEGIES

Analysis of your matches

Focus on observing if all aspects of the style of play that you have been training, are transferred to the match; either at a positional level, in player movements, phases of the game with the ball, phases of the game without the ball, set pieces, etc. It can be given in two ways.

Analysis during a football game

At this time, you should perceive the greatest number of situations in real time. **This is the most difficult analysis because the emotions of the game have their role**, and we tend to miss many details due to the dynamics of the game.

However, if you focus on carefully observing what happens at a global level, you can make decisions based on what the opponent does. Sometimes we have to adjust something in the formation or small details to modify the game.

For example, if the opposing striker goes deep to look for the ball in intermediate areas (between midfielders and centre-back) where he normally receives the ball alone, could a centre-back follow him? Can a midfielder follow him? How do we solve this situation? The solution depends on what you think is best based on the characteristics of your players.

Another example, your defenders cannot come out in control of the ball because the opponent presses with many players: can we alternate with direct play so that in the following actions they doubt whether to press or retreat? Where should we hit and why? Where is the free space that we can take advantage of?

These are actions that can be considered in matches and details that can change the dynamics of the game. More positional examples can be given that require changes in the formation or to the initial game plan, the important thing is that you must perceive if your team is suffering in attack or defence to try to counteract it.

Sometimes you are going to be right, other times you are going to be wrong and at other times the change will be made too late. Each game is unique, but I assure you that you will learn **if you focus on the details and stop watching the games as just another spectator**.

Post-match analysis

I recommend that you record the matches of your team if this is within your means. I know it is complicated in amateur football, but if you have a camera and a tripod, or if you can, it would be advisable that someone could record it trying to have the largest possible shot of the field or as many players as possible from the position where the ball is.

Most of the time, the perspective on the field is very different than when you see your team on video. **It makes you more objective of the situations; you might understand your players' decisions in some cases and even change your opinion of the game.**

On several occasions we have recorded matches where the analysis at the end of the game was unfavourable, but when we watched it back we realized that we played better than it seemed. There were many actions that we had been training, only that, due to small nuances, the progression of the plays was not entirely good and it gave a different impression when we were on the field.

For this reason, the post-match team's analysis allows the correction of nuances or game plan in a better way. You can even use video clips

TRAIN TO COMPETE

and show them to your players so they can see themselves (this is interesting for them and it is easier to correct actions by observing the error).

Remember, the opponent of the following weekend will be different from the one you faced in that game, so they will not experience the same situations. However, there are many actions that influence the game plan and you can work to correct or modify those.

Analysis of rival teams

Now, what should we analyse about our opponents to take advantage?

Minute 0

If you are going to watch one of your next opponent's matches, it is ideal that you are there from the kick-off, that is, from the beginning of the match. Normally, all teams start with their game plan, but it can be modified depending on situations.

On one occasion I went to watch a rival. I arrived half an hour after the game had started and one of the players had been sent off in the 15th minute. That means that the game changed, they were not the same circumstances. The match had been conditioned and possibly the things that happened with one less player were not going to happen with equal numbers of players.

Similarly, substitutions or the scoreline often modify the analysis. It is not the same to see a match that finishes 0-0, as seeing a match that after 10 minutes the result is 2-0, since, normally, the team that is winning will tend to take more care to keep that result, risking less and the team that is losing is the one trying to offer and risk more.

Which rival, on which field and in what climate?

You must consider that, if you are going to see a mid-table team, when that team is playing the top teams and when that team is playing the bottom teams, you are not watching the same team..

Therefore, if your team is second in the table and they are up against the bottom side, it is normal that they do not play the same way against you. But, if you see them playing against the top team, they may possibly do something similar in your match. **The rival often conditions the style of play**.

The same goes for the field. It is not the same to play home or away in terms of dimensions. The pitch conditions, environment, being more or less conservative, etc., are determining factors. Likewise, if it is wet or very hot it influences the game.

Rivals do not usually drastically change the way they play, but those nuances can modify certain behaviours or patterns. You must take it into consideration.

Analysis of the opponent's game phases

During the game you must consider that the 4 phases of the game are going to take place:

Offensive phase or organized attack

Do they play combinative, or do they play direct? I mean, do they try to play from the moment they have the ball with short passes and move forward? Or every time they have the ball, do they hit it up the field and pass it? They could also switch between the two (mixed). **Take note of it to think about how you could go to press or if it is better to retract.**

TRAIN TO COMPETE

Analyse: who normally plays long and on which side? If, for example, you like to press high and the opponents always attack down the right with very good players in those attacking zones, force them to play from the left and attack from the other side. You are already conditioning their output. It may or may not work, but it is a way to counteract what appears to be the opponent's strong point.

See what formation and moves they use to attack: are they always looking for width or do many players come inside? Are the wing backs very high up? What do the forwards do? There are a lot of things; I'm just giving you some important general ideas to ponder.

Offensive transition

When the opponent recovers the ball, what do they do? They can initiate a counterattack or start a combinative attack.

You can see if they quickly seek to occupy spaces in attack or try to circulate the ball patiently. From there, you must think about how to counteract those actions when you can lose the ball, to try to recover it as soon as possible or to avoid letting them create dangerous opportunities.

Defensive phase or organized defence

How do they defend when you have the ball? In low, medium, or high block, if they push you up, if they retreat back, what do they do?

Each team has its own way of defending, although I confess that most do not work on it. Even so, in amateur leagues it is very common that they will pressure you and especially if your team plays combinative, but many times it is unorganized pressure.

Very few teams fall back, and if they do, you will have to adapt your attack.

This phase allows you to observe what formation they use to defend, where the spaces usually are to combine and find your players according to your style of play, if they separate the lines of defence with the midfield, etc.

Defensive transition

When, in the game, your opponent loses the ball, what actions do they perform? Do they press quickly? Do they retreat? In the moment they lose the ball and must move quickly to defend. **There may be mismatches in their defensive zones that you could take advantage of.**

For example, if their wing backs are very high while trying to generate an attack, you could think about what to do when you recover the ball in midfield or defensive zones. Your forwards might be unmarked towards the wings to take advantage of the spaces left by rival wing-backs, bearing in mind that, at the start of the race, they will be ahead of their immediate central defender. So, it might be a good idea to play in those areas after recovering the ball.

Analysis of your strengths and weaknesses

All teams have strengths and weaknesses. You can face rivals who, perhaps, have slow centre backs and you can try to play behind them, or who are very good in aerial duels, and you have to play more combinative, avoiding 1v1 with duels.

In addition, you can individually analyse some aspects such as the most dangerous attacking player, the defender who is the most difficult to beat, which midfielder creates the most danger with their passes, if the wing-backs have a lot of space in attacking zones, etc.

Analysing your strengths allows you to adjust some aspects of the attack to take advantage of it, or the way in which you will defend to try to nullify their strong points. **There is no certain science in any action. Let's say we're just trying to improve our chances of winning, but we know that in football anything can happen.**

Dead ball

Another aspect to take into account are set piece strategies. In amateur football, not all teams have elaborate plays, but some coaches do.

At corners or throw-ins, you can observe the movement patterns of the players to try to counter it or take advantage of it.

Unlike professional football, where teams have many set pieces and depending on the rival, they use one or the other, in amateur football it is usually different. Most of these teams have 1 or 2 and repeat them during the season or change them for the second leg. So, get ready, because in a game they will surprise you with a set piece; But, if you've seen it, you can foresee it.

Important

With the data you have from the analysis you have carried out on your rivals, you must take into consideration the most important aspects before transmitting it to your team. For example: their most common movements, their greatest attacking threats and defence, how we can counter them and how to take advantage of them in attack.

Your players can't receive so much information about the rival because they will not remember it. You must be precise, even though sometimes, unintentionally, we give more information than we should.

I remember Pep Guardiola's 2020 talk when he won the first leg of the Champions League against Real Madrid 1-2 at the Santiago Bernabéu:

"I look at the opponents as much as I can... The decisions I make are based on what they do... I have given too much information to the players, yes, but I have to look at it as much as possible because I have to get to know them"[1].

We know that this is Guardiola and he has the ability to analyse all his rivals' matches without leaving his house. But the idea is clear: knowing many phases of the team you face allows you to find that action that gives you the greatest advantage at some point in the game. So, **be precise in what you want to talk about with the most important things, adapting them to your style of play.**

---

1   See Link: *https://www.youtube.com/watch?v=mUsjkcjNpw0*

CHAPTER IX

NOW WHAT?

These final notes, by way of closing and conclusion, are intended to put in the words of the author a general appreciation of the work of a coach, their expectations in football, what has existed up until now on the field and some theoretical references to better study this great sport.

INTRODUCTION

Are you ready to compete? I'm sure you are.

Football each year offers you different experiences, emotions, sensations, and criteria. However, **the more you learn, the less you seem to know**. This is what training is about, questioning what you know at all times and then reinventing yourself.

You already know important aspects that allow you to control more factors in your training sessions and games, with the mission of being competitive by training only 2 days a week. Although, for all the ideas that I have given you, experience will allow you to resolve situations that are not written in any book.

Therefore, this book is not based on a single way of doing things, nor on training methods, nor on scientific analysis, **because what sometimes works with one group, may not work with another**. But knowing how to manage a group of players, being clear about the objectives, associating training with match situations and training a style of play adapted to the potential of the group all generate incredible progress.

You can't be alone with this. There are many books, guides, and information on this great sport, but you must know how to choose. There is so much information on the subject and a lot of it is ambiguous.

Even some time after writing this book, I may want to modify it to give it another point of view or simply delve further into topics that I have written; I am sure I will. But I am also sure that this information can add value to many coaches or future soccer coaches.

IDEAS AND BOOKS

Before learning more for yourself think: where is football going?

What are the new trends? How do they train in professional football? How has training in grassroots and professional football evolved? Reflecting makes you research to improve.

I recommend you read books related to "Tactical Periodization". **This is the form of training that I have used the most, although it is not the only way to do it**. But, if you don't know how it works, how are you going to know if you want to choose this way or not? You must compare teaching styles to be able to choose the one you like the most and that is only done with training.

I will mention some books that in my opinion as a coach you should read and learn from to understand how football is evolving today:

- *Periodización táctica vs periodización táctica*, Xavier Tamarit
- *Mi receta del 4-4-2*, Robert Moreno
- *La preparación ¿física? en el fútbol*, Rafel Pol
- *Cómo leer el fútbol*, Ruud Gullit

- *Pep Guardiola La Metamorfosis*, Martí Perarnau

Also, analyse teams today to see different styles of play and continue reflecting on this world of coaching. Teams in 2020 like Guardiola's Manchester City; Bordalas' Getafe; Chris Wilder's Sheffield United, who have been the surprise package with an interesting style of play in England; Klopp's Liverpool and Flick's Bayern Munich.

Of course, there are more teams to analyse, I just mentioned a few that are currently standing out. Also, there are teams to consider such as Koeman's Barcelona, which is beginning a new era this season (20/21); Simeone's Atlético Madrid; Conte's Inter Milan; Zidane's Real Madrid; Luis Enrique's Spanish national team of Luis Enrique; among others.

All these teams have had different evolutions and football moments. Their styles have had variations for years due to changes in players and coaches, but analysing them will allow you to understand which is the default style of play according to the characteristics of their players and their usual movement patterns in their offensive and defensive phases.

So, back to the initial question: now what? Now there is a long way to go if you like this wonderful sport. **No matter how much you know and learn, there will always be a lot more to know.**

However, beyond competing with an amateur team, the most important thing to keep in mind is:

- Adapt to the group you have (levels)…
- Work with passion…
- Be consistent with what you say and do…
- Transmit confidence…

And if you can make them enjoy the entire season of this sport, with that you will be a good coach.

CHAPTER X

FINAL COMMENTS AND BIBLIOGRAPHY

Like the previous chapter, other bibliographic references used that helped to present some ideas in this book are in the bibliography below.

Words of thanks are also attached to the reader and to all those interested in studying more about football.

IMPORTANT

Football theories are very broad, and everyone has different ways of implementing them. Football is not the same in Argentina as it is in Spain. I want to say that, with this book, I want to add something of value for all coaches interested in continuing to learn about this wonderful sport, but remember what I said at the beginning: doubt everything because there is no absolute truth.

If you liked the book, put into practice everything that seems interesting to you, observe the results, and then let me know. **Your opinion is essential to continue providing more quality information.**

Please leave me a review on Amazon and tell me what you think, that will help me keep improving. What did you like the most? Is there anything missing? Would you add or remove any part?

And, if you prefer, contact me by email: bracamonte15@gmail.com

BIBLIOGRAPHY

- Bruno Oliveira. "**Mourinho, ¿Por qué tantas victorias?**". (2011) – Ed. MC Sport.

- Carlos Lago Peñas. "**Cortita y al pie**". (2018) – Ed. Amazon.

- Carlos Lago Peñas. "**Mírame a los ojitos**". (2019) – Ed. Amazon.

- Carlos Lago Peñas. "**Ganar, ganar y volver a ganar… sin dejar de Educar**". (2018) – Ed. Amazon.

- Patricia Ramírez. "**Así lideras, así compites**". (2015) – Ed. Conecta.

- Rafel Pol. "**La preparación ¿física? en el fútbol**". (2015) – Ed. MC Sport.

- Robert Moreno "**Mi "receta" del 4-4-2**". (2013) – Ed. Futbol de libro.

- Xavier Tamarit "**¿Qué es la Periodización Táctica?**" (2009). – Ed. MC Sport.

Printed in Great Britain
by Amazon